To:_____

From:_____

Thank you
MOM

Published by Sellers Publishing, Inc.
Text and illustrations copyright © 2012 Sandy Gingras

Sellers Publishing, Inc.
161 John Roberts Road, South Portland, Maine 04106
Visit our Web site: www.sellerspublishing.com
E-mail: rsp@rsvp.com

ISBN 13: 978-1-4162-0685-9

10 9 8 7 6 5 4

Printed and bound in China.

Thank you MOM

by Sandy Gingras

SELLERS
PUBLISHING

Dear Mom,
Thank you for so many things:
for what you say
and what you do,
for who you are
and how you make me feel.
Thank you for being my

friend, my teacher and
my biggest supporter.
Thank you most of all
for your love.
I carry it with me wherever
I go...

Thank you for helping me put the puzzle together.

and
always
being
happy
to see
me.

Thank you for telling me to follow my heart.

Thank you
for pushing me
out on a Limb,

and
showing me
that I could fly

Thank you for
planting the seeds.

Thank you for
giving me the courage
to be myself.

Today, you are you, that is truer than true; there is no one alive who is youer than you!

Thank you for making me eat my vegetables.

When I fell off,
thank you for
saying, "Get right
back on."

Thank you for checking for

Thank you for teaching me that strength is not just about muscles.

Thank you for reading me the stories (some again and again).

Thank you for
Letting me
Lick the bowl.

Thank you for
being my friend.

Thank you for believing in me.

Thank you for being
my hero and showing
me that a woman can
be anything she wants
to be.

Thank you for
giving me
structure.

Thank you for chocolate chip cookies warm out of the oven.

Thank you for boosting me up when Life gets me down.

Thank you for

making me practice.

Thank you for
Saying,

"DO THE
BEST
YOU CAN."

Thank you for wrapping me in warm quilts on cold nights and saying, "You're snug as a bug in a rug."

Thank you for making Lemons into Lemonade.

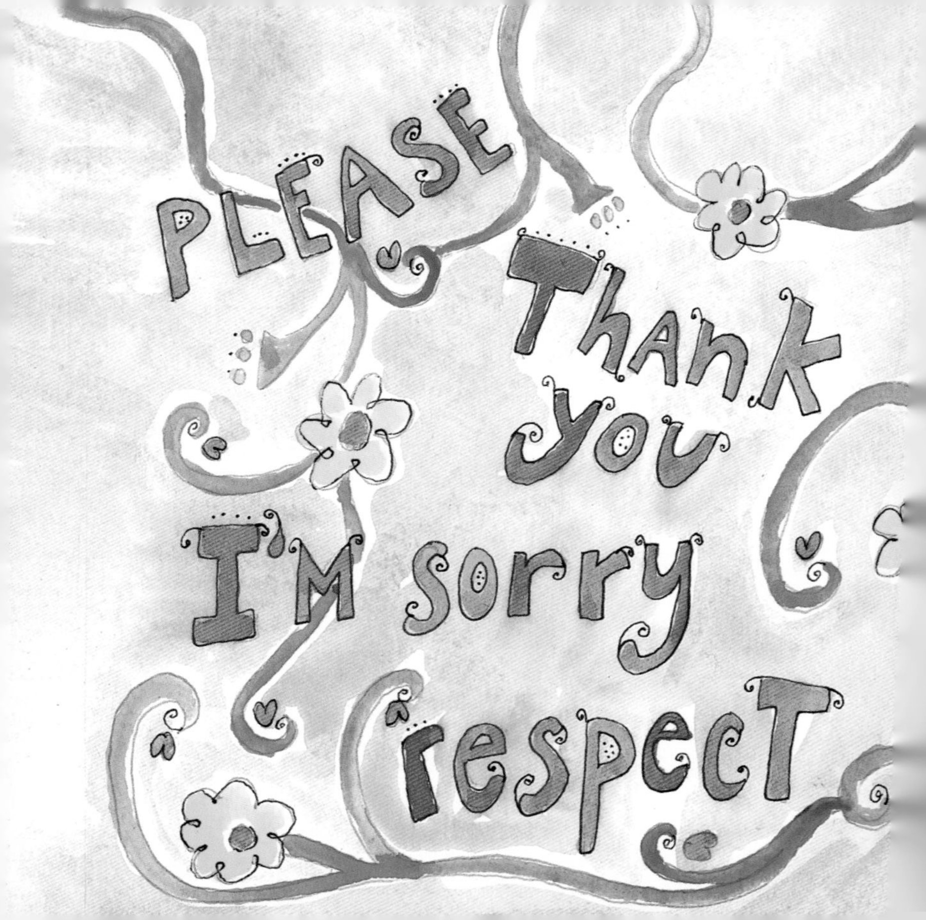
PLEASE
Thank you
I'M sorry
respect

Thank you for holding a safety net for me when I fall.

Thank you for
LuLLabies on
sLeepLess nighTs.

Thank you for telling me

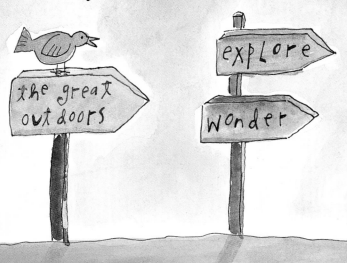

to go outside and play.

adventure

discover

Thank you for
Leaving a Light
on for me.

Thank you for comfort and hugs.

Thank you for

giving and giving and
giving and giving and giving and giving and giving
and giving and giving and
giving and giving and giving and giving and giving
and giving and giving and
giving and giving and giving
and giving and giving and